TEETH to TAIL of a

BookLife
freedom
Readers

GREAT WHITE
SHARK

By
Robin Twiddy

BookLife
PUBLISHING

©2022
BookLife Publishing Ltd.
King's Lynn
Norfolk PE30 4LS

All rights reserved.
Printed in Poland.

A catalogue record for
this book is available from
the British Library.

ISBN: 978-1-80155-130-4

Written by:
Robin Twiddy

Edited by:
Kirsty Holmes

Designed by:
Danielle Rippengill

BookLife
freedom
Readers

IMAGE CREDITS

All images are courtesy of Shutterstock.com, unless otherwise specified. With thanks to Getty Images, Thinkstock Photo and iStockphoto. Cover – Martin Prochazkacz, Ivan Kurmyshov, Andrey_Kuzmin, arka38. Boarder used throughout – arka38. Background Images – Ivan Kurmyshov, Andrey_Kuzmin, Song Heming, pirke, vovan. 2 – wildestanimal. 4 – Sergey Uryadnikov. 5 – Stefan Pircher. 6 – Martin Prochazkacz. 7 – SSaplaima. 8 & 9 – Tomas Kotouc. 10 – Alexyz3d. 11 – Masini. 12 – Alessandro De Maddalena. 13 – Alexius Sutandio. 14 – Palomba. 15 – Alessandro De Maddalena. 16 – Marc Henauer. 17 – wildestanimal. 18 – Sergey Uryadnikov. 19 – VisionDive. 20 – VisionDive, Petr Jilek, Ondrej Prosicky, Shane Myers Photography. 21 – Mogens Trolle. 22 – Elsa Hoffmann. 23 – solarseven.

CONTENTS

THE GREAT WHITE

There are around 440 known species of shark. Some are small, and some are large. Sharks have evolved and changed for millions of years to be the apex predators of the ocean. One of the most well-known species is the great white shark.

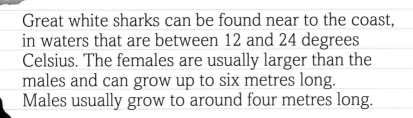

Great white sharks can be found near to the coast, in waters that are between 12 and 24 degrees Celsius. The females are usually larger than the males and can grow up to six metres long. Males usually grow to around four metres long.

TEETH

The great white shark has around five rows of teeth. The front row are larger and are used to bite prey. The teeth are large, triangular and serrated so they cut through flesh like a saw!

The great white shark can lose and replace around 30,000 teeth in its lifetime. Its teeth move like a conveyor belt. When one tooth is lost at the front, the ones behind move forward to replace it.

NOSE

Great white shark nostrils, called nares, are not used for breathing. They are only for smelling. The great white shark can smell well enough to detect a group of seals up to around three kilometres away!

The great white shark's nose is pointed like a cone, which helps it to move through the water. When it swims along, water moves through the nostrils. This allows it to detect blood and other things from its prey.

SKELETON

Shark skeletons are not made of bone like land animals' skeletons. Shark skeletons are made of cartilage. Cartilage is lighter and more flexible than bone. This allows the shark to float more easily.

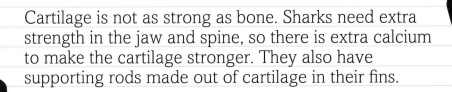

Cartilage is not as strong as bone. Sharks need extra strength in the jaw and spine, so there is extra calcium to make the cartilage stronger. They also have supporting rods made out of cartilage in their fins.

EYES

All sharks can see really well in dark or murky water. Different types of shark have different eyes that are adapted to how deep in the ocean they live. The deeper the shark lives, the smaller its eyes will be.

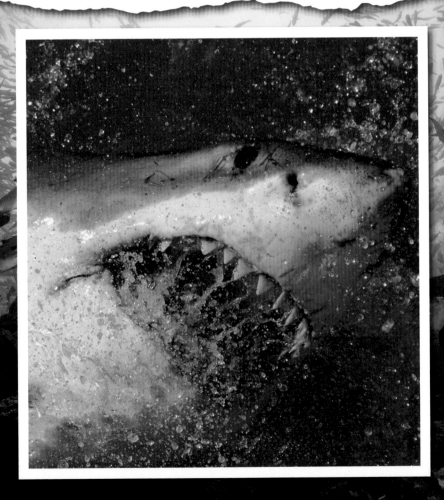

Part of the eye, called the retina, is divided into two parts. One is for seeing in normal daylight. The other is for seeing in low light. This means the shark can be a deadly hunter all the time!

FINS

All sharks have either four or five types of fin. The great white shark has five types. These are the caudal fin, the dorsal fin, the anal fin, the pelvic fin and the pectoral fin.

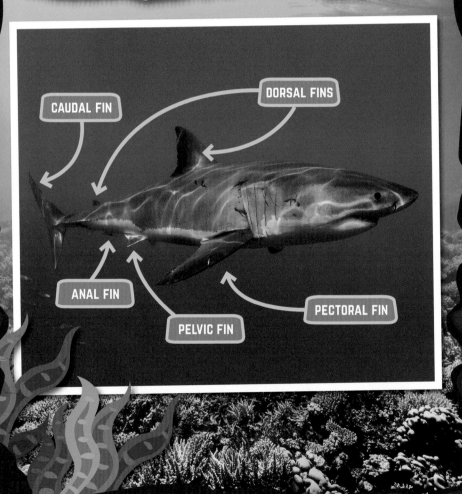

CAUDAL FIN

DORSAL FINS

ANAL FIN

PELVIC FIN

PECTORAL FIN

The different fins have different jobs that help a shark swim. When sharks swim with their dorsal fins breaking out of the water, it is called knifing. When a great white shark drops its pectoral fins, it is getting ready to move quickly.

SKIN

Shark skin is covered in tiny, tooth-like scales, called dermal denticles. The way that these are layered forces water past them, making the shark quick in the water.

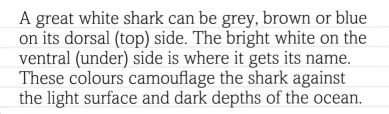

A great white shark can be grey, brown or blue on its dorsal (top) side. The bright white on the ventral (under) side is where it gets its name. These colours camouflage the shark against the light surface and dark depths of the ocean.

TAIL

The tail fin is called the caudal fin. The shark uses this fin to speed up and slow down. The great white shark's caudal fin is roughly the same length at the top and the bottom.

The great white shark uses its powerful tail to propel itself to speeds of around 56 kilometres per hour by moving it from side to side. The even, crescent-shaped caudal fin gives the shark a lot of control over its movement.

FOOD CHAIN

The great white shark is an apex predator, which means that it is at the top of its food chain. It eats smaller fish (including sharks), dolphins, porpoises, whales, seals, sea turtles and sea birds.

Sharks have special organs called the ampullae of Lorenzini which pick up electrical signals. Electrical signals make the heart beat. The great white shark's ampullae of Lorenzini are so powerful that they can detect the electrical signal of an animal's heartbeat.

LIFE CYCLE

The great white shark is ovoviviparous. This means that the babies grow inside an egg, but then hatch whilst still inside the mother. This takes about 11 months.

Baby sharks, called pups, are quite large and a female can have between two and ten at once. Males are fully mature and can breed from around nine or ten years old. Females mature at around 14 to 16 years old.

QUESTIONS

1: How many rows of teeth does a great white shark have?

2: Why is the great white shark's nose pointed like a cone?

3: What is the fin on the tip of the tail called?
a) Back fin
b) Rudder fin
c) Caudal fin

4: What does apex predator mean?

5: Can you think of any other types of shark? Make a list of all the sharks you can name.

BookLife
freedom
Readers